Woolly Mammoth

Written by Ron Wilson
Illustrated by Doreen Edwards

Library of Congress Cataloging in Publication Data

Wilson, Ron, 1941-
  Woolly mammoth.

  (The New dinosaur library)
  Summary: Presents information on this Ice Age creature and follows a young mammoth through his first year to his first mating.
    1. Mammoth—Juvenile literature.   [1. Mammoth]
I. Title.
QE882.P8W55   1984   569′.6   84-8380
ISBN 0-86592-203-9

Rourke Enterprises, Inc.
Vero Beach, FL 32964

Diplodocus

Pteranodon

Woolly Mammoth

Woolly Mammoth

Allosaurus

Hypsilophodon

Ichthyosaurus

It was cold. The earth had been covered by snow and ice for a very long time. The young woolly mammoth plodded around in search of food. The cold did not bother the creature. Its thick woolly coat protected it from even the harshest of weather.

Today the youngster plucked a few leaves from a willow tree. The best leaves were higher up on the branches. It was too much of an effort to reach up and strip them off.

He looked around. There was some food on the
bushes around about him. He turned to these. He
trumpeted a greeting to another mammoth which fed
close by. His neighbor called back. The herd was
scattered over the plains. Soon they would be coming
together to move south as winter approached. As the
mammoths browsed contentedly, woolly rhinoceroses
grazed on the grass.

Something inside the young mammoth told him
that the time for migration was drawing near. This
would be his first journey south without his mother.

No new leaves appeared on the trees. So, he had to move around to find enough to eat. Suddenly everything went dark. The mammoth looked up to see the first snows of winter drifting from the skies. Within minutes the trees and bushes were covered with a blanket of white. The snowstorm was short-lived. A weak, watery sun broke out from behind the clouds. It didn't stay long and another shower swept across the plains. The mammoth stopped feeding and ambled off to his nightly resting place.

During the night heavy snow fell, the flakes clinging to the creatures' woolly coats. As dawn broke the older members of the herd woke first. They were restless, and disturbed the rest of the herd. The young mammoth knew that it would soon be time to move south. The snow lay thick on the branches.

The older members set off, led by an elderly bull. They fed as they went.

The young mammoth was on his own. His mother now had other young to watch. He recognized her as she guided a much younger and smaller offspring on its way.

They were surrounded by hills. Snow lay everywhere. It had settled on the branches of the willows. The mammoth used his tusks and trunk to shake the snow so he could feed.

The young mammoth heard the familiar call of a woolly rhinoceros. He looked around him. There were many woolly rhinoceroses tearing at the rough grass. They were heading south too. The snow showers came more often. There was less sun and it was colder. The temperature seldom rose above freezing point.

Overhead large flocks of birds were also on their way south. Sometimes they landed on the trees to look for seeds. They were noisy and quarrelsome.

The herd of mammoths was now several hundred strong. They stopped for short periods, feeding on the fir and willow trees which sprang from the snow covered landscape.

The elderly bull leading the herd was having
trouble keeping the animals together. The young
mammoth heard a terrible noise. He hurried forward to
see what was happening.

The leader had been challenged by a younger
male. They were locked in combat. The young
mammoth looked on from a safe distance.

The rest of the herd had stopped. None tried to interfere in the battle. The conflict was brief. The old bull fell to the ground exhausted. He moaned gently and then was quiet. The challenger prodded the creature with his tusks. There was no response. The new leader trumpeted loudly to celebrate his success. The younger males assembled around him, answering his calls. The older members were more cautious, keeping their distance.

The new leader moved more quickly. Competition for the few leaves was increasing and it was first come first served. The young agile mammoths did better than their older relatives. Already some of these were dying, their bodies lying stiffly in the snow.

The herd was startled by a loud noise. Woolly mammoths and rhinoceroses stopped feeding. In the distance two woolly rhinoceroses were engaged in combat. They were fighting over the sparse grass.

The battle became intense. As if this were some kind of signal many other rhinos started to fight.

Although the young mammoth moved nearer he didn't get too close in case the rhinos attacked him. One old rhino fell to the ground. It writhed for a few minutes and then was still.

The trek south was uneventful except for the occasional fight. Food became even scarcer. More old mammoths and rhinos died. The young mammoth passed many dead bodies. Several weeks later they arrived at their winter home. The winds blew and the snows came.

The young mammoth knew that he was old enough to find a mate. Already he was looking around. Like him, all the other young males were thinking of mates.

Winter passed very slowly. Eventually the weather became warmer. The sun could be seen for longer periods as the days progressed. It was time for the mammoths to move back north again. The males already had their eyes on the few young females in the herd. Fighting for them would come soon enough. Although the young mammoth didn't look forward to combat he knew this was the way it was.

The journey north took many weeks. There was more food and the creatures fed frequently. The trees were showing their new coat of summer green.

The woolly mammoth knew from the landmarks that they were nearing their summer quarters. He trumpeted with excitement. A call which was taken up by many of the other creatures.

He tried to make his way to the front of the herd. Because he was young his place was near the back. The older mammoths prevented him from overtaking them.

At last they were home. There was much calling and shouting. The older mammoths were beginning to pair up. Some had already had their mates for many years.

The young mammoth had already spotted the unattached females. He made his way toward one of them. He called gently but she did not respond. He called again. This time his call was heard by another young male who threw out a challenge. The young mammoth charged at his opponent. At the same time the other young mammoth came toward him. The two retreated and charged again, trumpeting loudly.

After numerous attacks the young mammoths were exhausted. The challenger was ready to give up. But the young mammoth knew there had to be a winner; He called loudly to his opponent that he was challenging again.

Snorting loudly their small tusks became locked in conflict again. The young mammoth fought, but was soon wounded by his opponent. He was weakened and he withdrew. He knew he had to look for another female quickly.

He watched a female pulling leaves from a tree. He moved gently toward her. Within earshot he let out a quiet, friendly call so that he did not attract the attention of other males. There was no challenge. He moved closer toward the young female. He trumpeted gently; she answered his call.

The two mammoths stayed together until it was time to mate. They ate their fill from the willows and munched contentedly on the small shrubs.

Interesting facts about . . .
the Woolly Mammoth

The body had a very thick coat and up to 3 inches of fat just beneath the skin. The fat helped to keep the creature warm. It also provided it with a supply of food during the winter months when plants were difficult to get at.

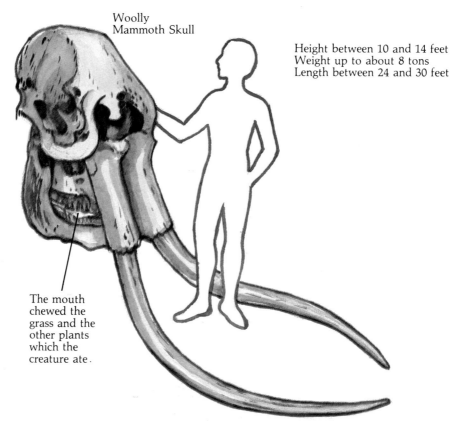

Woolly Mammoth Skull

Height between 10 and 14 feet
Weight up to about 8 tons
Length between 24 and 30 feet

The mouth chewed the grass and the other plants which the creature ate.

The skull of a Woolly Mammoth compared to a human

The Age of Mammals

Small mammals were alive when dinosaurs roamed the earth. No one is quite certain why dinosaurs died out. Some scientists think it could have been a change in the climate. Others have said that there might have been a major disaster, like a comet crashing into the earth.

With these large creatures out of the way, the mammals could develop. It took many millions of years.

The woolly mammoth lived during one of the ice ages. When scientists named it, they called it *Elephus Primigenius.* This means "first born elephant". Scientists called it this because when the fossils were discovered they thought it was a very early kind of elephant, but this was not correct. Other fossil remains which have been discovered show that it was one of the later elephants. Many other elephants had been on the earth before the woolly mammoths appeared. The first true elephants had lived millions of years before the woolly mammoth.

Creature of the Ice Age

There were Ice Ages which lasted for 200,000 years. When this happened the earth was covered with a coat of ice. Plants did grow and the woolly mammoth was able to feed on them. The temperatures were very low, however. To overcome these conditions the woolly mammoth developed a very thick coat of hair. It was a long shaggy coat. To keep the animal warm in these very cold conditions, there were two layers to the coat.

Where did they live?

The remains of woolly mammoths have been found in the northern parts of Asia, America and Europe. They lived in these countries from about the middle of the Pleistocene (1,800,000 to 10,000 years ago) until the end of that period. The last of the woolly mammoths probably died out about 10,000 years ago. The Pleistocene was the last period in the Cenozoic era. It is because mammals became the main creatures on the earth during the era that is often called the "Age of Mammals".

How do we know about the Mammoth?

We know about most animals which lived in the past because of the fossil remains which have been found. Much of what has been written and drawn has been pieced together. There has also been a great deal of guesswork. In the case of the woolly mammoth the situation is different. Although much of the ice disappeared at the end of the last Ice Age, there were still parts of the world which were very cold. They have been very cold since that time. During the Ice Age, mammoths died and were trapped in the ice. The ice has preserved them. Instead of just having bones to examine, as we do with most extinct creatures, whole mammoths have been discovered. With most prehistoric animals we have to guess what the skin looked like. It is very different with the woolly mammoth. Because whole mammals have been preserved, we can look at the hair and the tusks. In fact, we can look at all the body!

What did they eat?

Although they were large creatures, woolly mammoths fed on plants. They ate willow, fir, and alder leaves. They also ate the leaves from bushes. We know what the woolly mammoth ate because complete dead animals have been found in Siberia. When the stomach contents were examined many different kinds of leaves were found. Woolly mammoths probably used their tusks to clear snow from the ground so that they could get at their food.

What was the earliest elephant like?

The earliest elephants were small. They were like pygmy hippopotamuses or pigs. They grew larger as new species evolved over a long period of time. One of the largest elephants was the imperial mammoth which measured about 13 feet at the shoulder. The woolly mammoth was about 10 feet high.

Why did the mammoths become extinct?

No one is quite sure why the woolly mammoths became extinct — died out. Various suggestions have been made. It could have been due to changes in the climate. When the woolly mammoth lived it was during one of the Ice Ages. The ice gradually melted and the earth got warmer. This could have affected the woolly mammoth. Man also appeared on the scene. He might have hunted and killed the creature. It is also likely that man moved into the places where mammoths had lived. Man would have used some of their feeding grounds to grow his crops. The woolly mammoths would have been driven out with nowhere to go.

Things to do

Try and make a list of the animals which have become extinct since the woolly mammoth disappeared. Which sort of animals living today are most like the woolly mammoth? Can you think of reasons why our modern elephants don't have thick coats?

Draw a picture of a woolly mammoth. Then draw pictures of modern animals to scale. Make a picture with your cut outs.

Use a cardboard box. Cut out the front. Paint the inside and put in trees and bushes made from cardboard and paper. Use pipe cleaners and paper mache to make models of the woolly mamoth and the woolly rhinoceros. Put them inside the box.

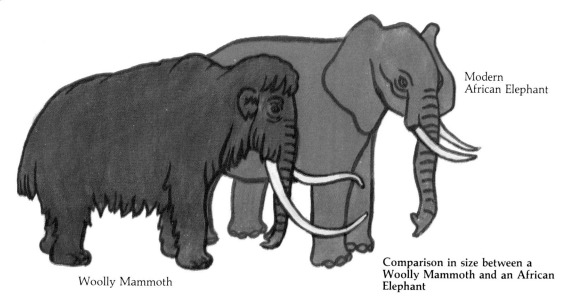

Modern
African Elephant

Woolly Mammoth

**Comparison in size between a
Woolly Mammoth and an African
Elephant**